Original title:
Lush Lines

Copyright © 2025 Creative Arts Management OÜ
All rights reserved.

Author: Ryan Sterling
ISBN HARDBACK: 978-1-80566-648-6
ISBN PAPERBACK: 978-1-80566-933-3

An Ode to Expansive Embrace

In gardens wide, the plants all cheer,
They dance in leaves, with joy sincere.
A squash debates, who wears the crown,
While cabbage rolls, then falls right down.

The bees in chorus, quite absurd,
They buzz and hum, it's really heard.
A dandelion's wish, it flies so high,
Yet lands smack down, oh me, oh my!

Enfolded in Nature's Palette.

Oh, palette bright, of veggies bold,
Each shade is something to behold.
Carrots boast their vibrant hue,
While broccoli shouts, 'Look at me too!'

The peppers wear their shiny coats,
In spicy stunts, they gloat and boast.
With onions crying just for fun,
And radishes that race, then run!

Verdant Whispers

In leafy chats where secrets lie,
A fern will giggle, not shy.
The thyme is sly, with wit so spry,
While mushrooms giggle, oh my, oh my!

The ivy climbs, with tales to spin,
Of how a beetroot wore a grin.
It's silly, yes, but don't you see?
In nature's jest, we all agree!

Silk Threads of Green

The vines weave tales of spending spree,
Plucking lunch from trees like a jubilee.
Tomatoes blush, they've got the flair,
While asparagus stands tall with care.

Peas play tag in their green brigade,
With radish cheers, a grand parade.
And as they laugh, the sunbeams wink,
It's quite the scene, more fun than you think!

Emergence of Springs

Bouncing buds on every tree,
They giggle in the gentle breeze,
A rubber ducky floats nearby,
Quacking at clouds in the sky.

Silly socks cling to the grass,
Dancing with a dandelion's sass,
A frog in shades croaks a funky tune,
Underneath a smiling moon.

Emerald Tides

Waves of green crash on the shore,
Seaweed noodles, who could ask for more?
Crabs in bow ties do the cha-cha,
While seagulls critique the salsa.

Surfboards painted like a clown,
Riding highs and tumbling down,
Fish in flip-flops start a race,
Chuckling as they splash with grace.

Interwoven Dreams

Stitches of laughter in the night,
Quilts of joy take off in flight,
Kites made out of careless schemes,
Catching winds of hopeful dreams.

A patchwork giraffe on parade,
With polka dots that never fade,
It trips, it slips, yet wears a grin,
In its world of yarn, it's a win!

The Fertile Canvas

Colors splatter, paint it bright,
A sprout that plays peekaboo each night,
The canvas tickles with a brush,
A dance of colors, a joyful rush.

Sunflowers sporting wacky hats,
Conduct a symphony with the bats,
Colors giggle, hues high five,
Artistry buzzes, pencils alive!

Elysian Fields

In fields so bright, where daisies play,
The cows all gossip, night and day.
A tumbleweed rolls by with flair,
The sheep hold parties, unaware.

The rooster sings a silly tune,
While pigs are dancing under the moon.
With nature's pranks, they never tire,
Each creature's whims spark endless fire.

The Art of Thicket

In tangled woods, the squirrels scheme,
Crafting traps like they're on a dream.
A rabbit hops, it's quite a sight,
And walks straight into a tree's delight.

With branches bent like painted brush,
The raccoons create art in a rush.
What madness lies within this green?
A canvas wild, yet so serene.

Verdancy Unveiled

In every sprout, a secret glows,
The weeds have campfires, who really knows?
With smiles wide, the ferns do sway,
While daisies giggle at the fray.

The ants throw parties in the dirt,
With tiny hats, they jump and flirt.
Nature's humor, sharp and keen,
The playful jesters of the green.

A Dance of Branches

Up in the trees, the branches sway,
In rhythm with the wind's loud play.
A parrot steals the show with flair,
He's quite the joker, without a care.

The owls hoot laughter from their perch,
As squirrels prepare for their great search.
With every sway and rustle, they bring,
Joyful mischief, nature's fling.

Vibrance in the Shadows

In the corners where plants do play,
Spider webs dance in a quirky ballet.
Ferns wear hats made of morning dew,
They giggle as sunlight bids adieu.

Green buddies gossip in the midday light,
Arguing over who grew the most bright.
Caterpillars strut in a leafy parade,
Their outfits, quite stylish, are all home-made.

The Flourishing Tangle

Vines are interwoven in a jolly twist,
They whisper secrets no one can resist.
A chubby squirrel dons a leafy crown,
Claiming the title of the best-dressed in town.

A dandelion giggles, a whimsical sight,
Blowing wishes into the soft night.
The bumblebee buzzes, a comedic flight,
Sipping on nectar, it's quite the delight.

Canopied Majesties

Tree branches wave, throwing shade with glee,
   Singing of summers and the buzzing bee.
  A grasshopper yo-yos from limb to limb,
    Telling tall tales on a sunny whim.

  Ivy wears sneakers, looking quite cool,
While mushrooms giggle, breaking every rule.
   Banana peels slip them into spins,
    In this leafy realm, everyone wins!

Glimmers of Growth

Sprouts stomp around in their fancy shoes,
Claiming new territory, singing the blues.
With every inch, they throw a grand fête,
Celebrating growth, it's really first rate.

Buds pop like popcorn in a sunny spree,
Nature's ruckus, oh so carefree.
The blooms bring laughter, a colorful jest,
In this garden realm, who grows the best?

The Dance of Growing Shadows

In the garden, shadows sway,
Dancing in a goofy way.
A sunflower spins, quite a sight,
While the daisies giggle in delight.

Trees wear hats made of leaves,
A squirrel's party with no reprieves.
They twirl and leap, oh what a scene,
In a world of clumsy green.

Rabbits hop in oversized shoes,
Chasing breezes, singing blues.
With every step, they trip and fall,
In this shadow dance, fun for all!

When night falls, they share a grin,
As shadows gather, the fun begins.
A moonbeam whispers a secret shy,
And the garden echoes a joyful sigh.

Flourishing Echoes of Silence

In a quiet place, whispers grow,
Where daisies gossip, 'Did you know?'
A butterfly flutters with great flair,
While the ants march, unaware.

The silence speaks, a funny tune,
As mushrooms sway beneath the moon.
It's an odd ballet, quite bizarre,
With crickets chirping, 'We're the stars!'

When raindrops fall, they start to prance,
Puddles form and invite a dance.
In each splash, a joke to share,
As petals giggle, dancing in air.

The echo of laughter fills the night,
As fireflies join, glowing bright.
In the calm, they find their beat,
In whispers soft, the fun's complete.

Vibrant Hues in Wandering Dreams

In dreams where colors brightly play,
Crayons laugh and sing all day.
A purple cat with polka dots,
Dances with orange-gowned robots.

Green giraffes wear funny ties,
As rainbow fish swim in blue skies.
A pink elephant plays the flute,
While dancing squirrels wear cute boots.

In the distance, laughter rings,
From bouncing clouds with fluffy wings.
They tickle stars and chase the moon,
In this vibrant, bustling tune.

With every stroke of bright delight,
The dreams get wilder in the night.
In colors bold, the fun unspools,
In this land of whimsical rules.

Radiant Threads Through the Meadow

In a meadow where sunbeams dart,
Worms wear shades, it's quite the art!
Grasshoppers strum on blades of green,
In a band of silly, loud routine.

Butterflies flutter with a wink,
While daisies tease with every blink.
A gentle breeze whispers a jest,
In this thread of joy, they're at their best.

Ladybugs race on tiny cars,
While bumblebees sing to the stars.
Every flower joins the fray,
In a colorful, chaotic ballet.

With laughter twirling on the wind,
The meadow thrives as joy rescinds.
Through radiant threads, they weave their cheer,
In this patch of fun, all is clear.

Echoes of Eden

In the garden where we hide,
The fruits are plump, come take a bite.
But watch the bees, they'll take a ride,
And buzz around in pure delight.

The apples giggle on the trees,
With cheeky smiles, they wave their leaves.
The carrots chat with bumblebees,
While playing tricks, oh what fun thieves!

A cabbage winks, as if to say,
'You're looking lost, come join the play.'
With every turn, the greens array,
A salad feast, we call it day.

So let us roam in joy and cheer,
With veggies dancing, let's not fear.
For every laugh, the fruit's sincere,
In Eden's charm, we shift to gear.

Bountiful Curves

In a land where tomatoes grow,
With roundness that's a show-off's glow.
They twist and twirl in sun's warm glow,
Declaring, 'Hey, we steal the show!'

The cucumbers, long and sly,
Dare to flirt, as they pass by.
They slink and slide with a winked eye,
While peppers blush and wonder why.

A dance of peas, in pods they clash,
In green attire, they make a splash.
With beans that stretch and take a sash,
They're quite the fun-loving, bold stash.

So join this veggie masquerade,
With funny shapes, no plans to fade.
In curves of crunch, let's all invade,
This joyful feast that nature made.

The Opulent Canopy

Underneath this leafy dome,
Where shadows play, we start to roam.
Each branch a laugh, a funny poem,
In nature's house, we feel at home.

The squirrels gossip, quite the chat,
While birds on branches think they're fat.
A crow that caws, 'Hey, look at that!'
With tales of seeds and where they sat.

The vines are twirling, green and spry,
With every twist, they flirt and fly.
In leafy rooms where laughter's high,
We find our hearts are light as sky.

Let's toast to trees with quirky bark,
That make the forest sing and lark.
In canopies of joy we embark,
Where humor blooms and leaves a mark.

Meadows of Enchantment

In meadows wide, the daisies dance,
With petals bright, they take a chance.
Each flower sways, a quirky prance,
   Inviting hearts to join the romance.

The bumblebees wear silly hats,
   Polling nectar, oh what spats!
They zoom around like chatty brats,
And giggle loud—can you believe that?

The butterflies, in colors bright,
Flap by with all their wings in flight.
They tease the blooms, oh what a sight,
   In joyful chaos, pure delight.

So here we laugh, in sunny fields,
With nature's charms, our heart it yields.
In meadows both, the magic shields,
   A funny tale, that joy reveals.

Tangled Melodies

In the garden where gnomes dance,
Hats on heads, they spin and prance.
A snail's slow race with a flirty bee,
Who knew nature could be so silly, whee!

Chickens chuckle as they strut,
Wobbling around in a playful rut.
A frog jumps high to reach the sky,
While ants compete—oh my, oh my!

The breeze plays tricks with a dragonfly,
Dizzying loops that make you sigh.
A squirrel twirls on a branch so low,
Oh, what a show, come watch it grow!

Under moonlight's cheerful glance,
The critters gather for a dance.
With giggles and squeaks, a merry chase,
In this garden, joy finds its place.

Oasis of Verdure

In a patch where the weeds have taken charge,
A raccoon plays piano, oh so large!
Mice tap dance on the old wood stump,
While the resident cat gives an unfunny grump.

A pot of herbs sings a jolly tune,
Especially when it's kissed by the moon.
Chives crack jokes, basil rolls its eyes,
Cilantro giggles at the hidden pies!

Rabbits bounce with curious flair,
Chasing shadows without a care.
The lettuce waves a leafy hello,
As cucumbers plot a silly show!

The sun sets low on this veggie spree,
The plants unwind, bubbling with glee.
Each sprout's a friend in this vivid blend,
An oasis of laughter that will never end.

Swaying Silhouettes

At dusk the wild grass starts to sway,
With shadows dancing in a cheeky play.
A raccoon pirouettes near a tall tree,
While the wind joins in, wheeling carefree.

Fireflies blink with mischievous grace,
As the moonbeam winks—who'll win this race?
A lonely crow tries to steal the show,
But a crowbar of laughter takes the glow!

The daisies giggle in soft twilight,
While crickets chirp with all their might.
Even the moon snickers in delight,
At this wacky scene that feels just right.

So watch as the night begins to hum,
With playful whispers and throbbing drum.
Nature's stage is set and wide,
In this night's antics, come take a ride!

Verdant Canopy Above the Rest

In a forest where the squirrels play,
Leaves dance like acrobats all day.
Branches wave with a cheeky cheer,
Nature's shenanigans make us leer.

The vines are tangled, a playful mess,
Plants gossiping, oh what a stress!
Moss whispers secrets on tree bark,
As I chuckle at a bird's loud quark.

Flowers wearing hats so bright,
Bees buzzing by, a comic flight.
Through this green, hilarity flows,
In this canopy, laughter grows.

Chipmunks waddle with tiny snacks,
As shadows stretch on their funny tracks.
Sunbeams tickle the forest floor,
In this leafy theater, we all adore.

Nature's Flourish in Blooming Time

Buds popping like confetti, oh what a sight,
Petals unfurling, pure delight.
Daisies donning shoes so white,
In nature's ball, it's a funny fight.

Bees in tuxedos, on a sweet spree,
While butterflies dance with glee.
Roots tugging gently, feeling their worth,
In this grand comedy of earth.

The daisies argue about who's the best,
Poppies just giggle and jest.
A panorama of colors, a cheerful play,
In floral antics, we find our way.

When blossoms wear their brightest grin,
And ladybugs bob, a whimsical spin.
Every petal prances, every bud chimes,
Nature's laughter echoes in these rhymes.

Intimate Blooms Beneath the Sun

Under the sun, the flowers swoon,
Petal gossip in the afternoon.
Tulips giggle, they just can't hide,
In this sunny spot, laughs coincide.

Lilies whisper tales of grace,
While daisies trip, they set the pace.
Bumblebees play hopscotch with flair,
In intimate gardens, without a care.

Sunflowers stretch to show their height,
With faces that beam, pure delight.
Every bloom sways in joyful spins,
In this sunny band, laughter begins.

Frogs croak tunes; with rhythm they croon,
As flowers sway, under the moon.
In simple charms, the earth unites,
In those intimate blooms, our joy ignites.

Textured Tapestry of the Wild

A canvas woven with colors bold,
Nature's humor, a story told.
Grasses tickle the toes we tread,
As crickets chirp jokes in their head.

Mushrooms pop like umbrellas bright,
In this playful world, laughter takes flight.
Fern fronds wave, a playful salute,
While flowers giggle, in fruitless pursuit.

A tapestry twists; a squirrel doth prance,
While ladybugs invite us to dance.
In tangled chaos, there's lots of fun,
In nature's gallery, every day's a pun.

Vines embrace with a teasing grip,
As butterflies swirl in a cheery trip.
In this wild gala, joy is gleaned,
In every texture, life's humor is dreamed.

Whorled Harmonies

The snail slid down the garden wall,
Thinking he was running, after all.
With style, he danced on leaves so green,
But sneezed and fell—what a silly scene!

Bumblebees buzzed with a heavy sound,
Complaining loudly, 'We're earthbound!'
They jiggled and jived in the air so bright,
Chasing each other, what a thrilling sight!

The flowers giggled in hues so bold,
Their petals whispered secrets untold,
They shared a joke with a fluttering breeze,
'This one's a bouquet, but who cut the cheese?'

In the sun's embrace, the critters pranced,
Each little creature had its wild dance,
With nature's orchestra playing a tune,
Under the watchful eye of the moon!

The Lattice of Life

In the garden, weeds wear crowns of green,
They think they're stars in a leafy scene.
While veggies tremble, hiding from the sun,
"Watch out!" they shout, "Here comes the fun!"

The carrots wiggle; the broccoli bows,
Turnips tell stories of gardenowls.
But cucumbers slip on a brushy dance floor,
Shrieking in laughter, "Oh, not again—more!"

Tomatoes blush as they grow so round,
"I'm a fruit, not a vegetable!" they resound.
While parsnips whine about being unchic,
Sprouts giggle back, "Hey, can't take a peek?"

In this lattice, friendships intertwine,
With dirt on their sleeves, they sip elder wine.
Each creature here queries, "What is our fate?"
"Just grow with a grin, and don't be late!"

Shades of Abundance

The carrots donned their finest hues,
Orange and green, sipping morning dews.
Meanwhile, the radishes staged a play,
"Turnip or not, who's our next prey?"

Peas in pods argued about their song,
"We're the best voices; you can't go wrong!"
Yet beet greens chimed in with a snicker,
"Hate to break it, but beetroot's quicker!"

Herbs laughed loudly at their neighbors near,
Roasting old pollens without any fear.
"Basil, don't chew the chives outta shape!"
Sneaky thyme grinned, "I'll give them a cape!"

In their patch, laughter spills like rain,
Fruits and veggies form a comical chain.
Together they thrive in a vibrant embrace,
Creating a world of mischievous grace!

Leafy Legacies

The ancient oak told tales of old,
Of squirrels that stole, as they bickered bold.
"Nature's a circus," the oak would sigh,
As leaves dipped low, reaching for the sky.

Maple trees dressed in colors so bright,
Gave fashion tips with a cheeky slight.
"Don't wear brown!" the aspens would yell,
"Unless it's autumn, then all will swell!"

Vines twisted round in a playful embrace,
Tickling flowers with a gentle grace.
"Who's the fairest?" a petal would tease,
About face and form, in the teasing breeze.

And when folks come by to sit and compare,
The whispers of nature, they'll always share.
"Laughter is timeless," the leaves would call,
"Join our grand waltz, it's the best of all!"

Brushstrokes of a Hidden Landscape

In the garden, secrets play,
A daisy wears a croquet hat.
Butterflies dance and sway,
While ants march out for tea, imagine that!

The broccoli is giving sass,
It's wearing sunglasses, oh so cool!
Radishes in a growing class,
They've made a real vegetable school!

Worms wriggle in their own parade,
Earthworms boast of dirt-filled fame.
Frogs join in the serenade,
While crickets strum their tiny game!

Flowers gossip, petals gossip,
Scenting the breeze with sweet delight.
A weed in need, oh what a tip,
Dares to invite the sun to bite!

Twisting Paths of Abundance

In the meadow, bumbles buzz,
Chasing each other like crazy fools.
Sunflowers wobble with a buzz,
Standing tall as nature's tools!

Squirrels hide their acorn stash,
Sporting tails like furry whips.
Rounding corners, oh what a dash,
As they dive and do little flips!

The carrots, shy, peek from their beds,
Hiding from rabbits with a lewd grin.
While cabbage grumbles, shakes its heads,
"Oh, what a world of leafy sin!"

Birds wear hats made out of twigs,
Dancing while chirping silly songs.
Around them twirls a team of figs,
Clapping along, it couldn't be wrong!

The Artistry of Overgrown Sprouts

Tiny sprouts, ambitious might,
Reaching for the sweetest sun.
Poking heads from morning light,
With dreams of their own green fun.

Lettuce giggles with the breeze,
Twisting its leaves with wild flair.
Zucchini strikes a pose with ease,
Flexing seeds like it has no care!

The peas plan a rolling race,
Against the beans, all fast in line.
Radishes fall, a comical chase,
As they bump heads and scoff in fine!

The garden's stage, a comical play,
Where vegetables frolic with might.
Oh, the silliness of the day,
In this patch, all feels so right!

Subtle Palette of Earth's Embrace

Colors swirl in earthy beds,
Painting soggy dreams in patchy plots.
Mischievous worms lift leafy heads,
As daisies giggle, tying knots.

Fungi sport their little caps,
Wobbling under a sunshine spree.
Cucumbers hide in silly naps,
While friends gather for a tea party!

The grass blades gossip all around,
Tickling at toes that wander by.
In this garden, joy is found,
As crickets serenade the sky.

Life's a canvas richly drawn,
With laughter flung in every hue.
Morning paints a laughing dawn,
In this wild plot of tangled view!

Rippled Canopies

In the shade of dancing leaves,
Squirrels act like little thieves.
They swipe my picnic, oh so bold,
And laugh aloud, or so I'm told.

Sunbeams tickle branches high,
Birds wear hats as they float by.
A napkin rustles in the breeze,
Turns into a kite with ease!

Raindrops tap, a playful beat,
As puddles form beneath my feet.
The world's a stage of whimsy bright,
Where every shadow plays with light.

Underneath the leafy crown,
My worries slowly drown.
With giggles shared, I play the fool,
In nature's prankster, open school.

The Buoyant Bough

A branch that swayed like it was dancing,
With acorns laughing and prancing.
The breeze embraced with cheeky flair,
While I just stared, caught unaware.

A crow in shades, so retro chic,
Complains to me, it's all quite bleak.
I shrug and share my snack of pie,
He quips, "Not bad for a small fry!"

Leaves giggle softly in sunny tune,
As daisies pretend to swoon.
Bees on missions, full of zest,
In nature's fun, they're always dressed.

So next you wander, look up high,
And join the fun, don't let it fly.
Each branch a jester, each leaf a mime,
In this big green comedy of time.

Nature's Wreath

A crown of daisies on my head,
The squirrels all giggle, countless threads.
They flaunt their tails, bright and spry,
While I sit here, looking shy.

The flowers whisper jokes so sly,
Telling tales of clouds that cry.
Each petal plays a clever role,
In nature's jest, they steal the show.

Bumblebees buzz with comic flair,
In a messy dance, all without care.
Their paths a scribble, wild and free,
Nature's humor, can't you see?

Through winding vines and leafy greens,
Laughter bubbles, bright and keen.
Here's a wreath to wear with pride,
In this garden where fun will abide.

Tangles of Time

A twisty vine that hugs the fence,
Says, "Life's a riddle, but it's intense!"
With roots that tickle along the ground,
It whispers secrets that astound.

Watch the ants in a single file,
Marching to work, they pause and smile.
"Join us now, abandon your clock,
In this tangled mess, come take stock!"

The wind, a joker, pulls my hat,
As I chase after it, how about that?
The sun bursts forth in shining beams,
Joining in on all our schemes.

So let the branches wander wide,
And let nature be our guide.
In tangled tales, we find the fun,
While laughing under the golden sun.

Flourishing Patterns in Stillness

In the garden, squirrels prance,
While daisies wear their sweetest glance.
The sunbeams dance, they twirl and sway,
Among the leaves, they softly play.

Bees in bow ties buzz around,
In their tiny suits, they make no sound.
With laughter bright, the flowers chat,
In this stillness, life's a spat.

The rhubarb waves, a friendly foe,
Pretends it's limbo at the show.
They twinklingly tie up their shoes,
In this garden, there's nothing to lose.

A frolicsome fern flips its fronds,
While daisies sway with silly bonds.
In patterns bright, they weave their jest,
In nature's realm, they're truly blessed.

The Symphony of Greenery's Embrace

Leaves are trumpets, oh what a sound,
In this orchestra, joy's all around.
The grass hums low, a gentle tune,
While daisies sway to the silver moon.

A bumblebee plays the drum, it seems,
Buzzing madly, fulfilling dreams.
Each sip of nectar, a sweet refrain,
In this symphony, we can't complain.

Violets chirp with a gentle glee,
"Come join our jam, sip honey tea!"
With petals vibrant, the laughter flows,
In this verdant ballad, fun just grows.

The willow winks, it's seen it all,
As the ivy scales the garden wall.
In each embrace, the humor's clear,
A riveting concert, bring on the cheer!

Feelings of Flourish in Heartbeats

Petals flutter like hearts in flight,
Waltzing softly in morning light.
Tulips giggle with all their might,
Claiming, "We're the stars tonight!"

The thorns attempt a grumpy pose,
While dandelions strike a pose.
"Watch us dance," the posies tease,
"We're made of giggles and summer breeze!"

Chirping birds on a whim decide,
To hold a race, oh what a ride!
From branch to berry, with flair they streak,
In every heartbeat, joy does peek.

The laughter sprouts like wildflower bliss,
In nature's quilt, you can't miss this.
With each small step, the fun does roam,
In the garden's pulse, we find our home.

Enchanted Strokes of Flora

With a brush made from willow's sway,
The painter blooms beneath the day.
Each blossom giggles, says "Look at me!"
Draped in colors so wild and free.

Tulip twirls in a dapper flair,
While poppies play without a care.
Every petal boasts its wear,
In this gallery, fun fills the air.

The ivy wraps in playful knots,
While sunflowers pose in quirky spots.
With laughter light, they hold their frame,
In this land, no two are the same.

A dainty design of petals bright,
In every stroke, sheer delight.
With artful hearts, they paint their dreams,
In this garden, nothing's as it seems.

Verdant Whispers

In the garden, a snail took a trip,
Wearing his shell, like a snug little ship.
He meets a grasshopper, who leaps with a grin,
"Why crawl so slow? Let the fun times begin!"

The daisies giggle, the tulips sway,
"Come join our dance! It's a flowery ballet!"
But the snail just chuckled, feeling quite spry,
"I'll take my time, no rush to comply!"

The sun pops in, wearing shades of delight,
"Hey garden dwellers! How's your day? Alright?"
The worms replied, with a wiggly cheer,
"Just digging for treasure, with nothing to fear!"

A butterfly flutters, "Oh, what a scene!
With petals and smiles, it's all so serene!"
The garden's a party, a bright little place,
Where each day's a giggle, painting joy on each face.

Silken Strokes on Canvas

On the canvas, a painter so bold,
Paints trees with a brush, dipped in marigold.
The clouds look at him with a playful sly,
"Why so serious? Just let colors fly!"

He swirls and twirls, with red and with blue,
"Just wait till it's done, you'll see the view!"
But a squirrel pops in, with a colorful scheme,
"Let's toss some acorns, and add to the dream!"

But the artist keeps turning, and mixing the hue,
"Acorns are nice, but I'm aiming for Q."
With a wink and a laugh, he flicks with a dash,
Creating a masterpiece, all in a flash.

When finished at last, oh what a sight!
Even the sun stops, with sheer delight.
"Let's paint the world, and make it a show,
With joy all around, let the fun colors flow!"

Emerald Veins of Nature

In a forest where chatter and laughter reside,
A bear in a bow tie took a brisk stride.
"Why look so dapper?" the fox gave a tease,
"I'm here for the party, let's swing from the trees!"

The deers prance in with a hop and a skip,
"Welcome to our bash! Will you take a dip?"
In a pond full of lily, the frogs start to croak,
Singing bad puns, as they make fun and joke.

The wise owl hoots, "Let's gather around,
With snacks in the woods, there's fun to be found!"
But a raccoon shouts, "I brought the popcorn!"
"Let's feast like kings till the breaking of dawn!"

As stars sprinkle down and the moon starts to glow,
Nature's grand party, what a fabulous show!
And there in the shadows, with each silly dance,
All creatures united, in a whimsical trance.

Curved Horizons of Green

On a hilltop, a parrot opened his beak,
With jokes about twigs, he gave it a peek.
"Why did the tree get a promotion, I say?
He was really good at branching out every day!"

A squirrel stopped short, with laughter so loud,
"I'll use that one later, it'll impress the crowd!"
The sun winked down, with a golden delight,
"Has anyone seen my bright golden light?"

A rabbit hopped in, with a basket of greens,
"Let's feast on the veggies, I brought some cuisines!"
With lettuce and carrots, they sat 'neath the shade,
Making munching sounds, in a leafy parade.

As shadows grew long, they made silly plans,
To twirl with the flowers, and dance with the fawns.
So here's to the giggles, the fun that we share,
In the curves of the meadows, joy's everywhere!

The Garden's Embrace

In the garden, the gnomes all dance,
Wearing hats that twirl in a merry trance.
Bees buzz by with a giggly hum,
While flowers laugh, "Oh, here they come!"

Worms wiggle with a comical flair,
In a soil party, with no need to care.
The daisies gossip, petals in a spin,
As ladybugs wear their spots with a grin.

A squirrel in shades, lounging on a leaf,
Sipping acorn juice, beyond belief.
With chirps and chuckles, the robin flies,
Cracking jokes under sunny skies.

Among the marigolds, a turtle struts,
In a party hat, oh what a nut!
The garden's embrace, where silliness blooms,
Is a riot of laughter that surely consumes.

Nature's Green Canvas

Brushes of leaves paint the sky so bright,
Where crickets sing tunes that ignite pure delight.
Hopping like frogs, the college kids play,
While dandelions sing, whisking cares away.

The sun paints a smile on the pond's gleam,
As fish splash around, living the dream.
Caterpillars curl in a chatty debate,
About who'll get wings to fly off to fate.

The trees chuckle, sharing shadows galore,
As squirrels run tracks like it's Olympic lore.
With twirls and spins, the petals rejoice,
In the art of green, nature finds its voice.

A picnic unfolds with ants in a line,
Bargaining crumbs, they say, "We'll be fine!"
Nature's green canvas, a riotous jest,
Where laughter and color put humor to test.

Shades of Serenity

In the shade of the oak, a cat naps awake,
Dreaming of mice that tease and create.
The wind whistles softly in playful delight,
As the flowers whisper, "Let's keep it light!"

A butterfly flutters with a wink and a nod,
Chasing bright blooms, feeling like a god.
With a tickle and tease, the petals all sway,
Creating a ruckus in their own silly way.

Frogs host a concert in a lilypad choir,
Singing their hearts out, never to tire.
While rabbits debate if they'll hop high or low,
In shades of serenity, the silliness flows.

With a pop and a giggle, the brook dances by,
Making splashes, catching sun in the sky.
In this realm where peace and jests intertwine,
Shades of serenity make humor divine.

Vines in the Breeze

Vines twist and twirl, with a cheeky grin,
Wrapping around trees as if they could win.
The sun peeks through leaves with playful eyes,
Whispering secrets that tickle the skies.

A raccoon dons a mask, ready for fun,
Raiding the garden, this rogue on the run.
With each little tumble, it looks so absurd,
Stealing the snacks, never shy to be heard.

Breezes carry jokes from the flowers so bright,
As daisies and tulips compete for the light.
The ivy giggles as it dances around,
Creating a scene that is utterly profound.

In this vine-filled world, laughter's the key,
With every twist, a new comedy spree.
Vines in the breeze—a whimsical cheer,
Where nature's laughter is loud and clear.

Surreal Touches of Vibrant Life

A frog in a top hat leaps with grace,
While flowers do the tango, in a flowery space.
Squirrels wear sunglasses, sipping on tea,
Dancing around, oh, what a sight to see!

The bees are buzzing in a wild parade,
While ants play trumpet, they're all getting laid.
Clouds giggle softly, whispering dreams,
As rainbows jog by in colorful teams.

Charmed Patterns in the Wilderness

The trees are gossiping, their branches entwine,
While mushrooms hold parties, all dressed up in fine.
Critters in tuxedos, a curious sight,
Chasing their shadows by the soft moonlight.

Bouncing rabbits wear bows, oh what a show!
While wise old owls are judging their flow.
Twinkling fireflies dance in the dusk,
Crafting bright patterns, as if in a husk.

Blossoming Gestures of the Forest

A flower waved hello with its bright, pink arm,
While vines told jokes, causing roots to charm.
The moss curls up, taking a sly nap,
Dreaming of butterflies playing a tap.

Bark beetles are drummers, tapping on wood,
While crickets compose, if only they could.
Leaves curl in laughter, rustling with flair,
As breezes carry giggles through the crisp air.

Lingering Scents of Fertile Earth

The soil smells like cake, or so they say,
As sprouting shoots giggle, 'We want some, yay!'
Worms in bowties slide to and fro,
Having a party below, don't you know?

The compost heap hums a jaunty tune,
While grasses sway slowly, beneath the moon.
Every plant's a comedian, spreading delight,
As roots tap-dance, until the morning light.

The Crescendo of Canopies

When trees are tall, they laugh so loud,
Their leaves do jig, like a dancing crowd.
A squirrel slips, with acorn flair,
And birds sing tunes from up in the air.

Beneath the shade, we play hide and seek,
A chameleon's trick, totally unique.
The sun peeks through, a naughty tease,
As branches sway, with effortless ease.

Ferned Memories

In a ferny maze, I lost my shoe,
The snails just laughed, said, "That's nothing new!"
I tripped on moss, a soft, green bed,
Said, "Help! I'm stuck!" while giggling instead.

With every step, a spore would fly,
My sneezes echoed, oh so spry!
The critters chuckled, what a sight,
As I danced on, with pure delight.

Blooming Enigma

A flower's face, all cheek and cheer,
Told me a joke that trapped my ear.
"It's all in the petals," it slyly said,
"Why do bees buzz? They all want bread!"

Roses rolled eyes, daisies in stitches,
Tulips joined in, their sweet little glitches.
In this garden, laughter resides,
With each dumb pun, the fun just abides.

The Green Tapestry

In tangled vines, a story spins,
Where clovers grow, the fun begins.
A caterpillar danced, quite the show,
Said, "I'll be a butterfly, just you know!"

As ferns and grasses made a quilt,
We laughed at the scene, of nature's wilt.
A picnic spread, with ants as the gate,
In this green world, we celebrate fate.

Cascading Colors in Quietude

In the garden, things collide,
A purple carrot, with pride.
The daffodils dance on a breeze,
Looking for partners, like bees.

A tomato tried to wear a hat,
But squished it flat—imagine that!
The lettuce giggled, turned to greens,
While radishes grumbled, about their jeans.

The bees are buzzing in a line,
Each buzzing tune tries to rhyme.
Meanwhile, flowers plot their charms,
Ending each day with open arms.

Oh, the carrots wish to swim,
In a puddle—yes, that's their whim!
While peas debate just who is best,
In this jolly garden fest!

The Weaving of Nature's Caress

A spider spins with great precision,
While grasshoppers hop with ambition.
The daisies hold a grand parade,
With tiny ants, in bright charade.

The sunflowers gossip with their heads,
About the squirrels and their spreads.
Can you believe the lengths they'll go?
To steal an acorn, what a show!

The clouds drift by, they wave and sway,
As we share gossip in the hay.
With each green blade, we softly sing,
About the silly things spring brings.

The sweetest fruits hang on thin threads,
While critters make their little beds.
They snicker as they try to sneak,
A berry snack—oh, what a week!

Embraced by Nurtured Growth

In the garden, there's always a clown,
A cucumber wearing a green gown.
This squash, so round, starts to roll,
Chasing a rabbit—oh, such a goal!

The carrots throw a birthday bash,
While broccoli makes a noise, a crash!
The radishes dance quite robust,
Declaring they love the garden trust.

A party unfolds, complete with cheers,
As tomatoes spread their joy through tears.
Each petal flutters, dressed to impress,
Nature's fashion shows, no time to rest!

So come join the fun in a fray,
With earth's quirkiest cast on display!
From zany roots to blossoms bright,
This garden brims with pure delight!

The Whispering Tapestry of Fruitful Fields

In the orchard, apples hush,
While pears are in a juicy rush.
The peaches giggle, sweet juicy puffs,
While cherries tease—are they all tough?

The winds tell stories, spin and sway,
About the figs who dropped today.
The grapevines weave a tale so grand,
Of mischief made in this vast land.

The corn, it stands, a tower high,
While pumpkins roll and ask, "Oh why?"
Dancing leaves begin to chat,
A secret world: who's really fat?

As harvest comes, a festival blooms,
When nature wastes no time in rooms.
So grab a fork, let laughter sing,
In fields where joy and bounty cling!

Rich Patterns of Earth

In fields where flowers pretend to dance,
The grasses whisper, given the chance.
Bees don their tuxes, buzzing with glee,
And ants throw a party beneath the big tree.

Mud pies get messy; oh, what a sight,
Worms hosting dinners in the pale moonlight.
The daisies giggle as they sway to the beat,
While the clovers plan snacks, a delectable treat.

Bobbling along, a rabbit shows flair,
Bouncing on blooms, without a care.
Squirrels debate which nut's a delight,
While butterflies prance, feeling just right.

All nature's mischiefs swirl all around,
In this playground where joy is unbound.
Let's raise a toast with lemonade cheer,
To the rich patterns of earth, oh so dear!

Sylvan Serenade

In the forest where fairies wear socks,
And trees stand tall in their witty talks,
Foxes in capes dance under the stars,
While owls hoot jokes in their old cars.

Mice with guitars strum near the stream,
Singing of nuts and a wild, sweet dream.
Bears trade their honey for a good laugh,
While rabbits debate the best vegetable path.

A raccoon juggles wild acorns so bright,
Squirrels all cheer, wishing for flight.
The brook gurgles softly, keeping it real,
As leaves flutter down with a twirly wheel.

The night air sparkles, full of delight,
Come hear the serenade, it's quite a sight.
Twirling through shadows, the laughs intertwine,
In the sylvan serenade, oh so divine!

Flourishing Echoes

In the garden where mischief unfolds,
Plants whisper secrets that nobody holds.
A crabapple giggles, its fruit looking shy,
While peas do their tango, oh my, oh my!

Roses send texts to tulips so bright,
As daisies critique the sun's shining light.
The carrots gossip about growing too steep,
While the broccoli dreams in a leafy heap.

Frogs in the pond are cracking a jest,
As dragonflies zoom for a speedy quest.
The daisies burst out, shouting cheer loud,
Creating a ruckus, making them proud.

In this garden, oh, what a mix,
Of whispers and chuckles, all sorts of tricks.
A chorus of laughter sweeps through the rows,
In flourishing echoes, anything goes!

Blossoms in the Mist

In the morning mist, where giggles arise,
The flowers are plotting with mischievous eyes.
Tulips wear glasses, acting quite wise,
While the daisies roll over, chuckling 'surprise!'

Butterflies gossip about flower trends,
Telling tall tales of their silky blends.
The morning dew drips like giggles on grass,
As a snail in a shell takes a journey, so fast!

Bees dress in jackets, they're on a spree,
Trying to woo petals, like it's a grand tea.
The sun peeks through, with a chuckle and wink,
The garden erupts; oh, will it all sink?

In this playful world with colors aglow,
Where laughter rings out in a bright flow.
Blossoms in the mist, they prance and they twist,
In a funny embrace, they simply can't resist!

Nature's Woven Secrets

In the forest's tangled hair,
Squirrels plot the great affair,
Moss grows beards on ancient trees,
Whispers float on gentle breeze.

Rabbits dance in crazy circles,
Wiggly worms in fashion's hurdles,
Ladybugs wear polka dots,
While frogs croak tunes that hit the spots.

Bees gossip over sweetened tea,
Knowing where the flowers spree,
Dandelions sport a crown,
As butterflies twirl without a frown.

Nature laughs, a playful jest,
In every nook, it finds the best,
With every leaf and furry friend,
A punchline waiting 'round each bend.

Threads of Abundance

A spider spins with wild delight,
Hoping dinner comes in sight,
Crickets wear their finest shoes,
The moonlights shine on nature's crews.

Beetles strut with tiny pride,
On tiny roads, they giggle wide,
Caterpillars, when they feast,
Munch away, a boisterous beast.

Tulips wear umbrellas up high,
While raindrops slip and sideways fly,
Grass hoppers leap, their humor spry,
In this garden, laughs will never die.

From roots to leaves, a joke in play,
With gnomes that tip their hats each day,
In the wealth of green, joy abounds,
Nature's wealth, where laughter resounds.

Radiance in the Underbrush

Under leaves where shadows creep,
Foxes plot, but still can't leap,
Glowworms light their party bright,
While owls hoot with sheer delight.

In the thicket, moss feels grand,
As sleepy bears form a band,
Raccoons laugh as they steal pies,
With cake crumbs left for alibis.

Berries blush at sun's warm gaze,
Their sweetness sparks a berry craze,
Fireflies chat about their glow,
Even in darkness, jokes still flow.

Nature dances, a comic scene,
Amid the green, joy's evergreen,
In underbrush, where secrets play,
Life's punchlines brighten every day.

Dawning Green

Morning breaks with chortles sweet,
As daisies put on fancy feet,
Sunlight tickles every leaf,
While tree trunks flex—beyond belief!

Chirping sparrows crack a smile,
With witty tweets that stage their style,
Pickles grow in cucumber dreams,
As nature bursts at its seams.

Puddles splash with ribbits loud,
Frogs become their splashing crowd,
Dewdrops giggle on the ground,
Each glimmer shines where joy is found.

New life blooms in colors bold,
In laughter's grip, the green unfolds,
With every dawn, a playful jest,
Nature's humor knows no rest.

Unity in the Garden

In the garden, veggies play,
Radishes dance the night away.
Tomatoes whisper, 'What a sight!'
While cucumbers giggle in delight.

Carrots boast of their tall height,
While peas argue about their might.
"Not so fast!" a sprout will claim,
And laughter fills the garden frame.

Bumblebees buzz with a jig,
Worms cheer on, both big and twig.
Unity grows in sun and rain,
With flowers smiling through the pain.

So join the fun, don't be shy,
In this garden, spirits fly.
Each plant's a friend, it's only fair,
In a wild, green, floral layer.

Flourish and Flow

Watch the leaves do the cha-cha,
While stems sway like they're in a fiesta.
Petals play tag, round and round,
In this dance of color, joy is found.

Budding blooms with a twist and twirl,
Shaking off morning dew like a pearl.
Roots underground giggle with glee,
As nature's party rages free.

Pollinators buzz with a grin,
Joining the dance, they all fit in.
A waltz that's composed of pure delight,
With each new petal, the world feels right.

So raise your hands, let laughter bloom,
In the garden, there's always room.
For those who seek a bloomin' good time,
Join the melody, it's pure rhyme.

The Dance of Petals

In a patch where petals prance,
They swirl around in a colorful trance.
Sunflowers shout, "Come and see!"
While daisies argue, "No, look at me!"

A windy gust gives a playful shove,
As roses blush in a fit of love.
The lilacs chime, they're in the mix,
With poppies spinning their fancy tricks.

A tulip leaps with a joyful cheer,
"Come join the dance, it's magic here!"
Carpet of colors on the ground,
With every flicker, joy is found.

Their laughter weaves through air so bright,
Under the glow of the moonlight.
Join the dance, let your worries cease,
And twirl in this petal-filled peace.

Enchanted Greenery

In a world of shades, so bright and bold,
The greenest tales are yet to be told.
Ferns climb high, with leaves that fling,
While mossy carpets softly sing.

Frogs do flips in a playful stream,
While crickets join in, fulfilling a dream.
A squirrel hops with nutty grace,
In this enchanted, leafy space.

Shrubs gossip, plotting their spree,
While the flowers sip on honeyed tea.
"Just be yourself and let it show!"
Said the ivy, "Let's steal the show!"

So let us play beneath this green,
Where laughter echoes, and joy is keen.
In every leaf, a secret dwells,
In enchanted greenery, laughter swells.

Cascades of Life

In a garden where giggles bloom,
Waterfalls drip from a ceramic spoon.
Bumblebees dance in clumsy glee,
While daisies whisper, "Come and see!"

The flowers wear hats, quite the sight,
Petals flapping in sheer delight.
Sunbeams tickle the morning air,
As butterflies buzz without a care.

Pumpkins proclaim their secret dreams,
While carrots plot in stealthy schemes.
The cabbages giggle, quite absurd,
As they chat about the latest bird!

Life cascades like a comic show,
Where everything's funny, don't you know?
Each turn in the plot's a crazy twist,
In this garden, nothing's amiss!

Leafy Labyrinth

In a maze of leaves, surprise awaits,
Lost in the greens, oh, what a fate!
A squirrel quips, 'This way or that?'
While a rabbit suggests, 'Try under that hat!'

With ivy that giggles at every turn,
And bushes that wiggle, it's my concern.
A path of tangles leads to strange sights,
Where roses recount their wild late nights.

Behind every tree, a joke is winked,
Fungi dress up while the garden shrinks.
In corners, gnomes laugh, hiding from rain,
In this leafy labyrinth, joy so insane!

Come join the riddle, twist and glide,
In this playful patch where green things abide.
Each leaf a story, each stem a song,
In our leafy labyrinth, you can't go wrong!

Curved Terrain

On a hill that giggles and twitches,
Grass grows sideways, oh how it glitches!
With vines that tie up a wandering mouse,
And daisies that chant, 'Welcome to our house!'

The path is wobbly, it turns and bends,
A joyful journey where laughter blends.
With worms doing yoga beneath the ground,
And clouds that float, all upside down!

Grab your hat, hold on to your snacks,
In this curved terrain, watch out for the pranks!
Mushrooms joke with a smile so cheesy,
While raindrops giggle, oh so breezy.

Turning and twisting, oh what a ride,
In this amusing hill, we take in stride.
The world is a jest, let's sing out loud,
In our curved terrain, let's draw a crowd!

The Essence of Flora

In a pot where the green things tease,
Herbs are gossiping with the breeze.
A cactus boasts, 'I'm stuck in my ways,'
While a sunflower grins, 'I'll brighten your days!'

Roses are blushing, chatting in pink,
While dandelions plot, 'Well, what do you think?'
Lavender laughs, 'I smell quite divine,'
Making sure every bee's in line!

A fern flips its leaves, playing hide and seek,
With peonies joining in—oh, how they squeak!
In this garden, where funny is key,
Flora concocts fun, just wait and see!

So dance with the petals, sway with the blooms,
In the essence of flora, laughter resumes.
With every snicker and every cheer,
We celebrate nature, let's give a cheer!

www.ingramcontent.com/pod-product-compliance
Lightning Source LLC
Chambersburg PA
CBHW072141200426
43209CB00051B/241